EARTH

EARTH

OUR PLANET IN SPACE

SEYMOUR SIMON

SIMON & SCHUSTER BOOKS FOR YOUNG READERS

New York   London   Toronto   Sydney   Singapore

SIMON & SCHUSTER BOOKS FOR YOUNG READERS
An imprint of Simon & Schuster Children's Publishing Division
1230 Avenue of the Americas, New York, New York 10020
Text copyright © 1984, 2003 by Seymour Simon
All rights reserved, including the right of reproduction in whole or in part in any form.
SIMON & SCHUSTER BOOKS FOR YOUNG READERS is a trademark of
Simon & Schuster.
Book design by Mark Siegel
The text for this book is set in Goudy Old Style.
Photograph on page 24 courtesy of Chris Van Hans, all other photographs courtesy of NASA.
Every effort has been made to trace the copyright holders, and we apologize for any unintentional omissions.
We would be pleased to insert the appropriate acknowledgment in any subsequent editions of this book.
Printed in Mexico
2 4 6 8 10 9 7 5 3 1
Libr0ary of Congress Cataloging-in-Publication Data
Simon, Seymour.
Earth: our planet in space / Seymour Simon.—Rev. ed.
p. cm.
ISBN 0-689-83562-0
1. Earth—Juvenile literature. 2. Earth—Photographs from space—Juvenile literature. [1. Earth.] I. Title.
QB631 .S56 2003
525—dc21   2001031304

To my sister Miriam
and her husband, Bernie

You live on Earth. You may live in a city or in the country. You may live where snow falls or where it never snows at all. But wherever you call home, you live on Earth. We all live on Earth.

Earth is in space. Space is outside the layer of air that surrounds Earth. Here is how Earth looks from miles and miles out in space. The dark places are seas, and the brown places are lands. Some of the seas and lands are covered by white clouds. The large white spot at the bottom is the snow-covered land of Antarctica.

Earth is a planet. A planet is a large world that travels around the sun.

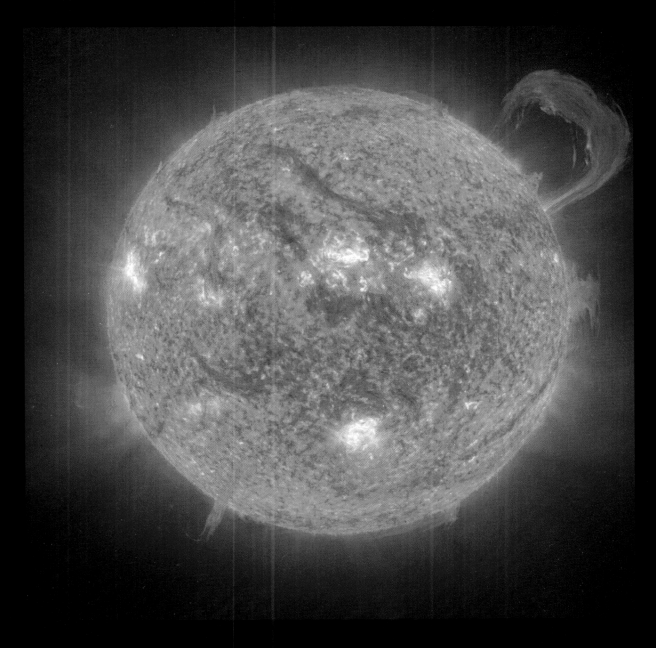

The sun is not a planet. It's a star a million times bigger than Earth. Light and heat come from the sun.

Earth is not the only planet that travels around the sun. Nine planets travel around the sun. Some of the planets are bigger than Earth, and some are smaller. Together, the sun and the planets are called our Solar System.

Here is a picture of the sun and the planets. Ten photographs were used to make this picture. The photographs are not to scale. The sun is six hundred times bigger than all the other planets put together. If the sun were the size shown in this picture, Jupiter would be about the size of the letter O and Earth would be about the size of the dot at the end of this sentence. The planets are shown in order from the sun. The top four are Mercury, Venus, Earth, and Mars. The next row shows Jupiter, Saturn, Uranus, Neptune, and Pluto. Some astronomers think that Pluto is an asteroid or comet rather than a planet. But many people still want Pluto to be called the ninth planet.

In this photograph Earth's shadow is traveling across the moon. Many years ago, people thought that the Earth was flat, but you can see that the shadow of Earth is of a curve. The shadow helped people learn that Earth is round. Today, scientists photograph and measure Earth from spaceships. They say our planet is shaped almost like a ball. It is very slightly pear-shaped.

In the photograph on the right you can see how Earth looks from the surface of the moon. Light from the sun falls on one half of the Earth at a time. One half of the Earth is light while the other half is dark. From the moon you can see the light side but not the dark side of Earth.

Earth is spinning all the time. It spins like a giant top. While you are on the light side, it is daytime. To you, when the light side spins away from the sun, it looks as if the sun is going down. Then darkness falls and it is nighttime. When the dark side spins toward the sun, it looks to you as if the sun is rising. Light comes to the side of Earth that has been in darkness and daytime begins.

But the sun is not moving. It is Earth that is spinning. We call that motion, Earth's rotation. It takes one day, or twenty-four hours for Earth to rotate once.

While Earth rotates once a day, it also travels around the sun in a path called an orbit. We call that motion around the sun, Earth's revolution. It takes Earth one year, about 365¼ days, to make one complete orbit around the sun.

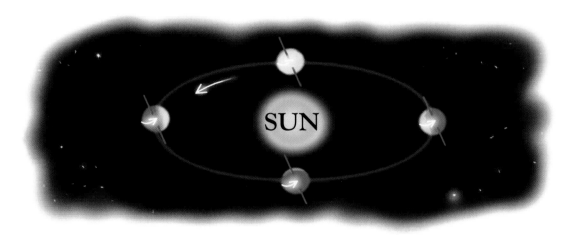

Earth's Orbit

Earth is about 93 million miles from the sun. If Earth were closer, it would broil. If the Earth were farther, it would freeze. The sun is just the right distance for the living things on Earth.

There is no planet that is the same distance from our sun, so there is no planet that has the same temperatures as Earth. As far as we know, Earth is the only one of the planets that has plants, animals, and people.

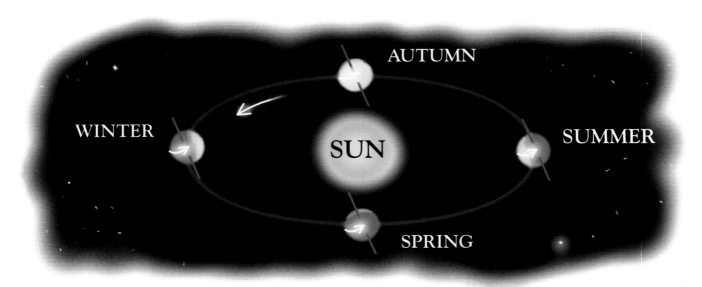

Seasons in the Northern Half of Earth

One half of earth has winter while the other half has summer. When Earth travels around the sun, it is tilted to one side. For part of the year, the northern half of Earth is tilted toward the sun. When this happens, the northern half of Earth has summer.

At that time the southern half of Earth is tilted away from the sun, so southern places have winter.

The seasons change. Winter changes into spring, which turns into summer, and summer changes into fall, which turns into winter. As Earth travels around the sun, sometimes the north is tilted away, and the northern places become colder. At the same time, the southern half of Earth is tilted toward the sun, and summer comes. As the year goes by, the place where you live on Earth warms up in summer or cools off in winter.

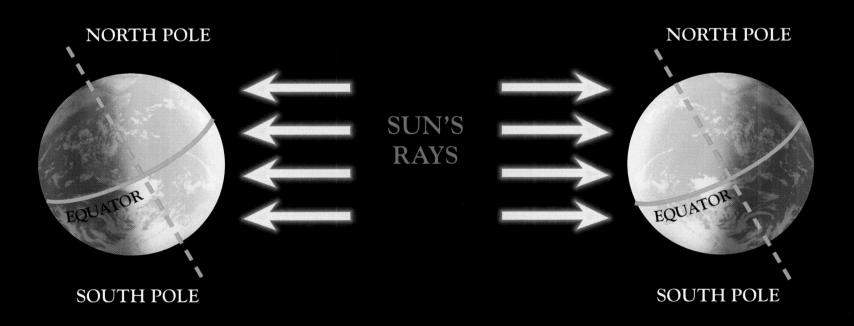

Earth has a blanket of air around it that keeps it from getting too hot or too cold.

The blanket of air is called the atmosphere. Earth's atmosphere is made of gases and bits of dust and water. The atmosphere helps make Earth a planet full of living things. No other planet has an atmosphere like Earth's.

Earth is like a giant magnet. The space around a magnet is called a magnetic field. Earth's magnetic field acts like a shield. It helps protect living things from dangerous radiation from the sun and space that can kill everything on Earth. The magnetic field sometimes makes colored lights you can see in the night sky. These lights are called an aurora. Here is a photograph of an aurora.

The surface of planet Earth is covered with land and water. This is a photograph of Lower California. These mountain ranges are mostly barren of vegetation and water, but the white places are caps of snow.

There is much more water than land on the surface of our planet. Oceans cover nearly three quarters of Earth.

The lands on Earth's surface are always changing. Here is a photograph of the highest mountains on Earth—the Himalayas in Asia. Mountains are pushed up by changes inside our planet. The Himalayas are still rising. The snow-covered mountains are over twelve thousand feet high. The dark line is a deep river valley. Over many years the river scraped deep into the land.

The surface of the land wears away. In winter, water freezes and becomes ice. The ice breaks up the rock and wears it away. Snow piles up and pushes down on the land. In this photograph you can see how snow and ice have worked to change the surface of the land.

People also change the surface of the land. They farm the land. They dig into the land and use the rocks and minerals they find. This is a photograph of Phoenix, Arizona.

Can you see the ways the land has been changed?

This is New York City. Millions of people live there in thousands of buildings. Yet this great city is just a tiny speck on Earth's surface. To an astronaut on the moon, which is Earth's closest neighbor in space, no signs of people can be seen.

People have dreamed of leaving Earth to explore other worlds in space. We have already landed on the moon. We have sent spaceships to explore the other planets in our Solar System.

We have also found other planets circling far-distant stars. As we learn about these planets, we learn about Earth as well.

All of us travel together through space. Our space-ship is called Planet Earth.